"Ready-made prayer services to help children appreciate the saints? Long have teachers awaited such a book! Gwen Costello keeps these mini-celebrations short and simple. She divides up the speaking parts so everyone gets involved and she gives us an index of feast days by month... In short, Costello knows precisely what teachers need before they walk into the classroom."

Page McKean Zyromski
Author of *Echo Stories for Saints and Seasons*

"In *Praying with the Saints,* Gwen Costello gives a gift to modern children that they desperately need: that of good role-models, which she presents in a creative and colorful array of lives of the saints from many walks of life. Actually, this book is a gift, not only to children, but also to families, to catechists, to classroom teachers, to home-schoolers, and to every corner of the earth where there are children and people who love them.

"The book contains an amazing amount of basic Catholic doctrine presented in attractive and very usable ways. The material goes hand-in-hand with the teachings in the *Catechism of the Catholic Church*: stories from Scripture, references to the Trinity, the Incarnation, the life of Jesus; also the eucharist, the beatitudes, and efforts for peace and justice, as well as prayer. And, all these great truths are presented in a single and attractive way through the lives of the saints."

Sr. Maxine Inkel, S.L.
Author of *100 Fun Ways to Liveler Lessons*

"The saints are real people, and our children deserve the chance to get to know and follow them. Gwen Costello offers us this opportunity in her book *Praying with the Saints.* She has created an easy-to-follow format with a meaningful prayer service followed by the children's response. This activity brings the life of the saint into the daily life of the children as it challenges them to imitate the virtues and qualities of that person. This book should be in the hands of every religion teacher of young children."

Gail Thomas McKenna
Author of *Models and Trends in Religious Education*

"A mini introduction to the saints for children, this prayer service manual provides a reminder that we as believers are never alone as it invites us to pray to and with the saints. An important inclusion to any Catholic school curriculum—lest we forget those so worthy of remembering."

Ginger Farry
Author of *A Teacher's Prayerbook: To know and love your students*

"Gwen Costello has added another implement to the catechist's tool kit with this delightful introduction to the saints for children. While saints are often presented as role models, rarely do the children learn that the saints wish to help us. In her exercises, Gwen teaches the children to ask the saints for help in their daily lives."

Ed Ransom
Author of *Saints for Our Time*

"Gwen Costello's choices for inclusion go beyond the familiar models as she accomplishes her goal of proving that the lives of the saints are worthy examples to follow. The selections are creative and challenging and call children (and teachers) to imitate the special qualities of each saint.

"With the brief introductions as a lure for further investigation, Costello's suggested prayer and action responses offer variety for children in today's culture. Imagine inviting a saint home as an overnight guest—a 'sleep over' with St. Brendan or St. Genevieve—and how that might impact a realization of the saint for all family members! The suggested activities are also valuable for community-building and exposing the children to values of justice found in Scripture."

Julie A. Hayes
Director of Christian Formation
St. Michael Parish, Exeter, NH

GWEN COSTELLO

PRAYING
WITH THE
SAINTS

30 Classroom Services

for Children

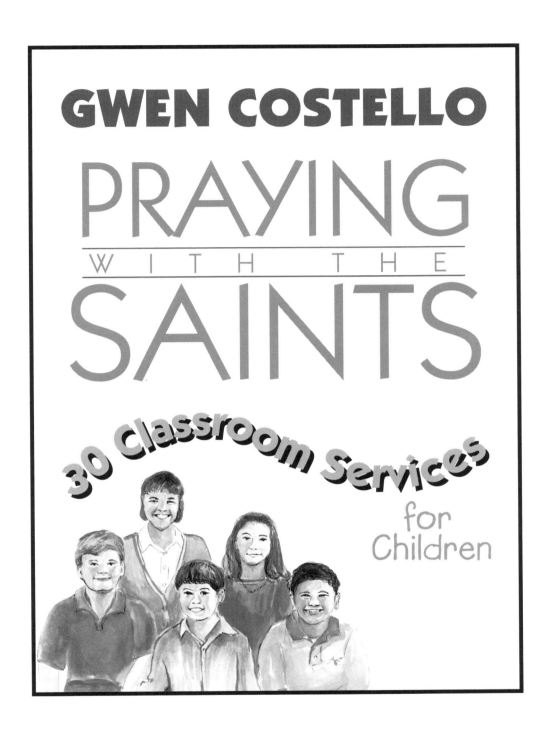

TWENTY-THIRD PUBLICATIONS
Mystic, CT 06355

Twenty-Third Publications
185 Willow Street
P.O. Box 180
Mystic, CT 06355
(860) 536-2611
(800) 321-0411

ISBN: 0-89622-982-3
Library of Congress Catalog Card Number: 99-71175
Printed in the U.S.A.

Dedication

For all the contemporary "saints"
in my life who have loved me,
guided me, and encouraged me
as I searched for ways
to proclaim the gospel of Christ,
especially Sr. M. Callista,
Sr. M. Perpetua,
Karen Crouse, OSF,
Sr. Kathleen McEleny,
Sr. Rosalie Bean,
and Mary Parzych

Contents

Introduction

I love the saints. I love their stories. I admire their deep faith, their devoted love, their hope when all seemed hopeless. I love it that no matter what the circumstances of our lives, there is a saint that we can look to for guidance, direction, and courage.

As a child, I attended parochial school, and so I grew up with the saints, so to speak. Children today don't necessarily have this experience. That's why I wrote this book, to introduce them to some of the church's greatest role models.

The saints do have something to say to children today and their lives are worth studying and imitating. Some of the saints have stories, legends, and myths that mix up fact and fiction, but for the most part there is something very real about even the most obscure saints: their faith. Saints were attracted to prayer, good works, and penitential practices because they believed that God was to be trusted, honored, and cherished. They believed that God sent Jesus to show us how to live, which primarily translates into service for others (see Matthew 25). Thus, their lives were given over to the service of others. By following Jesus, they entered into a close and personal relationship with God, one that characterized their lives.

These qualities and practices are contained in each of the prayer services in this book as well as in the "Action Responses" and "Optional Activities." I want children to meet the saints, to pray to and with them, to imitate their great qualities, and to reach out to others as they did.

The thirty saints represented here are from different cultures, different centuries, and vastly different backgrounds. They are a mix of young and old, male and female, but they all have qualities that children today can and should imitate. These qualities are the primary focus of the services in this book. You'll notice that I begin with Jesus, our foremost model, who is followed by Mary, whose whole life said "yes" to God.

What the services include

Each service begins with a brief introduction by the "Leader," a teacher or cate-chist. This is followed by a class prayer with "suggested prayer gestures." These are simple movements that all children can do, and should be practiced before the actual prayers are prayed. Most of the services use "Readers," children in the class who can read slowly and dramatically enough to be prayerful. Of course, you can adapt the number of readers to suit who is available to read. Some of the services have "Choruses" and "Side One/Side Two" parts, which means that different groups say different things. Simply divide the class into the number of groupings called for in the service, whether two or three. Again, a bit of practice beforehand will make the actual prayer time more meaningful.

After the class prayer service there is a "Prayer Response," a time for sponta-neous prayers. I suggest in each service that children pray for and about people with whom each particular saint worked: the poor, the hungry, the sick, children in war-torn countries, and so on. I also suggest that catechists and teachers invite children to pray for their own needs and those of their families, community, and parish. These spontaneous prayers are followed by a few moments of silent prayer.

I recommend that after each service children be invited to pray to the featured saint in their own words. I suggest that you give them an index card or something similar to write their prayer. You might think of alternate ways to have them do this prayer, and I encourage you to be creative.

The final element in each of these services is the "Optional Activity," something you can do to take each saint's message a bit further. These include games, guest speakers, role-play, discussions, and guided meditations.

At the back of the book, I list "Suggested Resources," should you want to explore the lives of these saints in more detail. You'll find a wealth of information in each of the resources listed, as well as some creative suggestions for sharing each saint's story. There is also an index which lists the saints by month, in chronological order of their feastdays.

Let me end where I began. I love the saints, and I will be delighted if the chil-dren in your classes learn to love them too as they pray these services and share these activities. This is where I leave off and your work begins. May it be for you and your class an enjoyable and spiritually rewarding experience.

ONE

Jesus our Savior

FEASTDAY: Christmas, the Baptism of the Lord, Sacred Heart, Corpus Christi, Transfiguration, Easter, Christ the King, and every day of every year

Leader   Jesus our Savior is our daily guide on our journey through life. He guides us at home, at school, and in all our everyday activities. We recall his words from the gospel: "Come be my followers, and I will be with you always" (John 14:18). Jesus always points the way for us toward doing the right thing as God's children.

Suggested prayer gesture: *Each time the Chorus parts are spoken, all should raise their hands in an upward gesture of praise.*

Chorus 1   Glory be to the Father and to the Son and to the Holy Spirit…

Chorus 2   As it was in the beginning, is now, and ever shall be, world without end. Amen.

Reader 1   God, our Father and Creator, be with us now as we think about and pray about ways to better follow Jesus. Open our minds and hearts that we may be good followers.

Chorus 1	Glory be to the Father and to the Son and to the Holy Spirit…
Chorus 2	As it was in the beginning, is now, and ever shall be, world without end. Amen.
Reader 2	Jesus, our brother and friend, we believe that you are with us, always calling us to do God's will: at home, at school, in religion class, and everywhere we go. Help us to follow you always.
Chorus 1	Glory be to the Father and to the Son and to the Holy Spirit…
Chorus 2	As it was in the beginning, is now, and ever shall be, world without end. Amen.
Reader 3	Holy Spirit, our friend and guide, help us to grow in holiness by praying for others, especially those in need, and by sharing what we have with others. Show us how to follow Jesus.
Chorus 1	Glory be to the Father and to the Son and to the Holy Spirit…
Chorus 2	As it was in the beginning, is now, and ever shall be, world without end. Amen.

Prayer Response

Invite the children to pray aloud for Christians all over the world, and especially for missionaries who are far from home. All can respond: "Jesus, blessed Savior, hear our prayer." Now invite the children to think of needs they and their families have and to offer these to God in a moment of silent prayer.

Action Response

As they leave class, make a cross on each child's forehead while saying: "(Name), may you follow Jesus today and always." Each can answer: "Amen." Encourage the children to pray to Jesus when they wake up in the morning and before they go to sleep at night.

Before the children leave, give each an index card on which is written: My Personal Prayer to Jesus. They can take the cards home to complete with help from their parents. Encourage them to say the prayer at bedtime.

Optional Activity

If possible obtain the name of a missionary, someone your class can write to from time to time. Explain that missionaries carry the message of Jesus to other lands, and they spend their lives helping others in Jesus' name. Encourage the children to pray for this missionary often, as well as for the people he or she ministers to and with.

TWO

Mary our Mother

FEASTDAY: September 8, December 8, January 1, and March 25

Leader	Mary, the mother of Jesus, is our mother too, and we can learn from her example. When good things happened to her, she praised God, saying, "I praise and rejoice in God, my savior." She had great faith and she will help us to grow in faith as well. Let us praise God as Mary did (read Mary's prayer in Luke 1:46–55). Through the centuries the church has given Mary many titles, among them, Mother of God, Mother of the Church, the Immaculate Conception, Our Lady of Sorrows, and Blessed Mother.

Suggested prayer gesture: *All should fold their hands when the Readers speak their parts.*

Right Side	We are happy to be God's chosen ones; we rejoice in our God.
Left Side	Holy is God's name, forever and ever.
Reader 1	Mary, our Mother, you were God's chosen one. God asked you to be the mother of the savior and

you said "yes." Help us to say "yes" to our parents and teachers today when they ask for our help and support.

Right Side   We are happy to be God's chosen ones; we rejoice in our God.

Left Side   Holy is God's name, forever and ever.

Reader 2   Mary, our Mother, help us to say "yes" to those in need by sharing what we can of our time and money. Help us to remember those who suffer by reaching out to them with love and compassion.

Right Side   We are happy to be God's chosen ones; we rejoice in our God.

Left Side   Holy is God's name, forever and ever.

Reader 3   Mary, our Mother, help us to say "yes" to God every day by being kind and courteous to one another and by doing our best at school and in religion class.

Right Side   We are happy to be God's chosen ones; we rejoice in our God.

Left Side   Holy is God's name, forever and ever.

Prayer Response

At this time, invite the children to pray aloud to Mary for their mothers, grandmothers, pregnant women, and for mothers throughout the world. All can respond: "Mary, our Mother, pray for us." Encourage the children to pray silently now for personal and family needs.

Action Response

Spend time as a class discussing ways that you might praise God more joyfully, as joyfully as Mary did, when you gather. Invite the children to create a prayer from themselves to God that says "yes" to God (as Mary's prayer said "yes").

Before the children leave, give each an index card on which is written: My Personal Prayer to Mary. They can take the cards home to complete with help from their parents. Encourage them to say the prayer at bedtime.

Optional Activity

Share with the children some of the titles the church has given Mary; for example, those found in the Litany of Loreto, which was compiled in 1558. (It is also called the Litany of the Blessed Mother). Have the children choose one of the titles and draw a symbol or picture based on it to share with others in the class and to take home to their families.

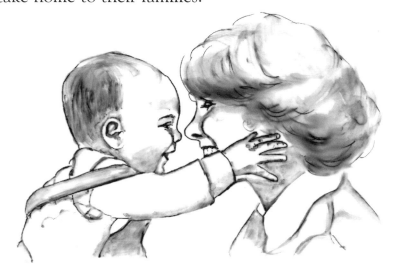

THREE

Martha of Bethany

FEASTDAY: July 29

Leader
Martha, the sister of Mary and Lazarus, was a holy woman, very devoted to Jesus. One time when Jesus visited her, she was fixing dinner for him, and she became upset by all there was to do. Jesus told her to slow down and spend more time listening and praying. We should follow this advice, too. Martha had deep faith in Jesus and believed that he could bring her brother Lazarus (who had died while Jesus was away) back to life. And Jesus did.

Suggested prayer gesture: *Everyone should hold hands and arms straight upward during the prayers said by All.*

Left Side
May we honor the holy name of Jesus.

Right Side
May we enjoy his friendship in this life.

All
And may we be happy in God's kingdom forever.

Reader 1
Loving God, we, like Martha, are too concerned with the little things in our lives. Help us to learn how to listen to you and pray.

Left Side   May we honor the holy name of Jesus.

Right Side   May we enjoy his friendship in this life.

All   And may we be happy in God's kingdom forever.

Reader 2   Loving God, teach us how to pray to Jesus, and then to listen in silence for his response.

Left Side   May we honor the holy name of Jesus.

Right Side   May we enjoy his friendship in this life.

All   And may we be happy in God's kingdom forever.

Reader 3   Loving God, strengthen our faith in the Holy Spirit, who is always with us, teaching us how to pray.

Left Side   May we honor the holy name of Jesus.

Right Side   May we enjoy his friendship in this life.

All   And may we be happy in God's kingdom forever.

Prayer Response

Encourage the children to pray aloud, especially for parents and home-makers throughout the world. All can respond: "St. Martha, pray for us." Invite the children to also pray for the special needs of their family and friends. Conclude with a moment of silent prayer.

Action Response

Encourage the children to stop at least once today for a spontaneous moment of prayer: before doing homework, before washing dishes, before taking out the garbage. Simply pray: "Jesus, help me to listen to you."

Before the children leave, give each an index card on which is written: My Personal Prayer to St. Martha. They can take the cards home to complete with help from their parents. Encourage them to say the prayer at bedtime.

Optional Activity

The gospels give us two images of Martha. The first is that she is busy about many things, but not about the things that really matter. The second is that she had a deep faith in Jesus and what he could do. Explain to the children that Martha needed to grow in her understanding of who Jesus was and what was necessary to follow him. Even good people can change for the better.

FOUR

Peter the Apostle

FEASTDAY: February 22 and June 29

Leader	Peter the apostle had great faith, but at first his faith was weak. When Jesus was arrested, Peter lied, saying, "I do not know him." Later, Peter was very sorry. Jesus forgave him and made him the leader of all believers. May our faith be as strong as St. Peter's.

Suggested prayer gesture: *As the Choruses recite the lines below, all should make a small cross on forehead, mouth, and chest (as at Mass when the gospel is announced).*

Chorus 1	We believe in God, creator of heaven and earth.
Chorus 2	We believe in Jesus Christ, our savior.
Chorus 3	We believe in the Holy Spirit, who dwells in our hearts.
Reader 1	Help us, loving God, to have deep faith like St. Peter. Help us to believe that you are always with us.
Chorus 1	We believe in God, creator of heaven and earth.

Chorus 2   We believe in Jesus Christ, our savior.

Chorus 3   We believe in the Holy Spirit, who dwells in our hearts.

Reader 2   Strengthen us, Jesus, that we might always act as God wants us to act, at home, at school, wherever we are.

Chorus 1   We believe in God, creator of heaven and earth.

Chorus 2   We believe in Jesus Christ, our savior.

Chorus 3   We believe in the Holy Spirit, who dwells in our hearts.

Reader 3   Holy Spirit, help us to remember that even when we fail, you are always with us, forgiving us and helping us start anew.

Chorus 1   We believe in God, creator of heaven and earth.

Chorus 2   We believe in Jesus Christ, our savior.

Chorus 3   We believe in the Holy Spirit, who dwells in our hearts.

Prayer Response

Invite the children to pray aloud for church leaders: the pope, their bishop, their parish priests, and other parish leaders. Pray as well for the global needs and concerns of the church. All can respond: "St. Peter, pray for our church." Conclude with a moment of silent prayer.

Action Response

The name "Peter" means "rock." As a class (if you can do this conveniently), go outside to find small stones or rocks and place them on your class prayer table as a reminder that God's love and forgiveness is rock solid. Encourage the children to ask St. Peter daily for the gift of deep and lasting faith.

Before the children leave, give each an index card on which is written: My Personal Prayer to St. Peter. They can take the cards home to complete with help from their parents. Encourage them to say the prayer at bedtime.

Optional Activity

Have the children search the gospels (in groups of three or four) for stories about Peter. Ask each group to discuss how it might present the story for others in the class, for example, through role-play, an interview, a letter from Peter to the class, drawings that tell the story in sequence, and so on. Encourage creativity.

FIVE

Mary Magdalene

FEASTDAY: July 22 and Easter

Leader Tradition tells us that Mary Magdalene was a sinful woman before she met Jesus. But Jesus forgave her sins and she became one of his most loyal followers. Jesus must have loved her very much for he appeared to her after his resurrection. Let us try to love and follow Jesus as Mary Magdalene did.

Suggested prayer gesture: *Everyone should bow when reciting the lines for All.*

Right Side May God bless us and keep us safe.

Left Side May God's face shine upon us and be gracious to us.

All May God look upon us kindly and give us peace.

Reader 1 Mary Magdalene was a known sinner, but Jesus looked beyond her sins to the love that was in her heart. Mary was sorry for her sins and Jesus forgave her completely.

Right Side   May God bless us and keep us safe.

Left Side   May God's face shine upon us and be gracious to us.

All   May God look upon us kindly and give us peace.

Reader 2   Jesus forgives our sins, failures, and weaknesses. He loves us, no matter what.

Right Side   May God bless us and keep us safe.

Left Side   May God's face shine upon us and be gracious to us.

All   May God look upon us kindly and give us peace.

Reader 3   May we be faithful and loyal followers of Jesus, and share our faith with others as often as we can.

Right Side   May God bless us and keep us safe.

Left Side   May God's face shine upon us and be gracious to us.

All   May God look upon us kindly and give us peace.

Prayer Response

At this time, invite the children to pray aloud for people throughout the world who are considered outcasts or sinners. (You might want to talk with them first about who they would put in this category and why.) All can respond: "St. Mary Magdalene, pray for us." End with a moment of silent prayer.

Action Response

Mary Magdalene was one of the first followers to meet the risen Christ after his resurrection. Share with the children the account of this meeting from John's gospel (chapter 20, verses 11–18), and encourage them to speak to Jesus often as friend to friend, believing that he calls them by name as he called Mary.

Before the children leave, give each an index card on which is written: My Personal Prayer to St. Mary Magdalene. They can take the cards home to complete with help from their parents. Encourage them to say the prayer at bedtime.

Optional Activity

Have a class lesson or discussion about sin. Explain to the children that while sin exists and each of us is a sinner from time to time, only God sees what is in a person's heart. Mary Magdalene was considered a sinner by the people of her time, and yet Jesus loved her as a friend. It was she who announced to the disciples that Jesus was risen.

SIX

Paul of Tarsus

FEASTDAY: January 25 and June 29

Leader   Paul, born in the Greek city of Tarsus, was Jewish and a Roman citizen. He was at first an enemy of Christians. Once when he was on the way to arrest a group of them, he had a vision of Jesus who asked: "Paul, why are you persecuting me?" Paul understood from this that Jesus lives within all who believe in him, and then Paul himself became a believer, too.

Suggested prayer gesture: *All should hold hands out, palms upward as Left Side /Right Side prayers are said.*

Left Side   Glory to you, O Word of God, giver of life and light.

Right Side   May the fire that burned in Paul's heart burn in our hearts, too.

Reader 1   St. Paul, pray for us that we might be faithful followers of Jesus, especially by showing love and respect for one another.

Left Side Glory to you, O Word of God, giver of life and light.

Right Side May the fire that burned in Paul's heart burn in our hearts, too.

Reader 2 May we be faithful followers by the way we act at home, in school, in religion class, in our parish, in our neighborhood, and with our friends.

Left Side Glory to you, O Word of God, giver of life and light.

Right Side May the fire that burned in Paul's heart burn in our hearts, too.

Reader 3 Pray for us, St. Paul, that we might be grateful for the great gift of our faith and gladly share it with others.

Left Side Glory to you, O Word of God, giver of life and light.

Right Side May the fire that burned in Paul's heart burn in our hearts, too.

Prayer Response

Invite the children to pray spontaneously for all the people in our world who are proclaiming the gospel. Use this response: "St. Paul, give us faith." If there are special needs in their families or among their friends, encourage the children to bring these to prayer, too. End with a moment of silent prayer.

Action Response

Share the story of St. Paul's conversion in the Acts of the Apostles (chapter 9, verses 1–30). Have the children take turns reading this account. After sharing reactions to this story, give each child a prayer card on which is written: "Dear Jesus, may the fire that burned in St. Paul's heart burn in our hearts, too." Encourage them to pray these words often.

Before the children leave, give each an index card on which is written: My Personal Prayer to St. Paul. They can take the cards home to complete with help from their parents. Encourage them to say the prayer at bedtime.

Optional Activity

Share with your class excerpts from one of Paul's letters to the early churches. (Though not all of these letters were written by Paul, all have been attributed to him because they contain his teachings and those of his coworkers in ministry.) Then ask the children to write a letter to the Christian community in their parish. What would they say to encourage people to be faithful followers of Jesus Christ? Have them share these letters with the class and then take them home to share with their families.

SEVEN

Perpetua

FEASTDAY: March 7

Leader Perpetua (died 203) was a wife and the mother of an infant when she was put in prison. When she refused to give up her Christian faith, she and her friend, Felicity, who was in prison with her, were put to death. Obviously, their faith was very, very strong. Both their names are sometimes mentioned at Mass.

Suggested prayer gesture: *All should raise open hands when reciting the All prayers.*

Left Side Jesus, you are the light of the world.

Right Side Those who follow you do not walk in the dark.

All Please give us your light of life.

Reader 1 Give us a strong faith, loving God, that we might always put Jesus first in our lives, always remembering his presence among us as Perpetua did.

Left Side	Jesus, you are the light of the world.
Right Side	Those who follow you do not walk in the dark.
All	Please give us your light of life.
Reader 2	Help us to be brave, loving God, as Perpetua was, so that we might be witnesses of faith for others.
Left Side	Jesus, you are the light of the world.
Right Side	Those who follow you do not walk in the dark.
All	Please give us your light of life.
Reader 3	St. Perpetua, pray for our class. Help us to grow in faith, so that we might truly and joyfully celebrate the presence of Jesus in our lives.
Left Side	Jesus, you are the light of the world.
Right Side	Those who follow you do not walk in the dark.
All	Please give us your light of life.

Prayer Response

Take time now to pray for all young mothers with children, especially mothers in countries where physicians and medicines are not readily available. The response is: "St. Perpetua, pray for all mothers." Invite the children to pray for their own mothers and grandmothers (or guardians) and end with a moment of silent prayer.

Action Response

Remind the children to pray for the gift of faith every day. If possible, teach them this act of faith: "Jesus, I do believe in you. Please make my faith strong and walk with me this day. Amen."

Before the children leave, give each an index card on which is written: My Personal Prayer to St. Perpetua. They can take the cards home to complete with help from their parents. Encourage them to say the prayer at bedtime.

Optional Activity

Many dioceses have a Catholic Charities office through which help is given to young pregnant women. If possible, have someone from your diocese talk to your class about the work the church is doing in this regard.

EIGHT

Lawrence

FEASTDAY: August 10

Leader   Lawrence (died 258) is one of the most well known of the early Christian martyrs. He was a deacon and when asked by the prefect (leader) of Rome to turn over the church's treasure, he gathered the city's poor and suffering and said, "Here is the church's treasure."

Suggested prayer gesture: *Everyone should make the Sign of the Cross as the All parts are prayed.*

All   To God the Father, Son, and Spirit, one in three,
be glory as it was, is now, and shall forever be.

Reader 1   St. Lawrence, you had special love for the poor and the sick, so much so that you called them the church's treasure. Help us to love and care for the poor as you did.

All   To God the Father, Son, and Spirit, one in three,
be glory as it was, is now, and shall forever be.

Reader 2   St. Lawrence, help us to share our money and our belongings with the poor. Help us to learn to do without things we don't really need so that we can help others.

All   To God the Father, Son, and Spirit, one in three, be glory as it was, is now, and shall forever be.

Reader 2   St. Lawrence, you were courageous in living out your faith, and were not afraid to die for the sake of Jesus. Help us to be strong in our faith, and never be afraid to say "I believe!"

All   To God the Father, Son, and Spirit, one in three, be glory as it was, is now, and shall forever be.

Prayer Response

Take time now to pray for your class' special needs, and invite the children to pray for the poor and the sick in their families, the parish, the neighborhood, the world. The response is: "St. Lawrence, pray for us." Conclude with a few moments of silent prayer.

Action Response

Give each child in your class an inventory list that includes such items as: shoes, shirts, games, toys, coats, hats, CDs, watches, etc. Invite them to take these lists home and fill them out. Tell them to especially note items they never wear or use. Then have them talk to their parents about the list. Is there something they could share with someone in need? At the bottom of the inventory list, include a note to parents suggesting that they encourage their children to give away and/or share items that others might need.

Before the children leave, give each an index card on which is written: My Personal Prayer to St. Lawrence. They can take the cards home to complete with help from their parents. Encourage them to say the prayer at bedtime.

Optional Activity

Role-play with your class some scenarios that involve being put on the spot to tell the truth, no matter what the consequences. What would the children do, for example, if they were with a group of friends who taunted or bullied someone, and then were asked who did it? What would they do if someone stole something and they were witnesses, and they were asked about the incident?

The point here is that being honest and taking a stand is not easy. Practicing virtue calls for courage and faith, the kind St. Lawrence had.

NINE

Sebastian

FEASTDAY: January 20

Leader Sebastian, an early Christian martyr (died c. 288), was an officer in the Roman army. When other officers learned he was a Christian, they turned him over to be punished. He refused to deny his faith in Jesus, and he was killed with arrows by the soldiers he once led.

Suggested prayer gesture: *All should make a scattering seed motion as the Chorus 2 lines are prayed.*

Chorus 1 Lord, make us instruments of your peace.

Chorus 2 Where there is hatred, let us sow love. Where there is doubt, let us sow faith.

Reader 1 St. Sebastian, you were very brave as a soldier, but even more brave as a follower of Christ. Help us to follow Jesus in everything we do.

Chorus 1 Lord, make us instruments of your peace.

Chorus 2   Where there is hatred, let us sow love. Where there is doubt, let us sow faith.

Reader 2   St. Sebastian, you gave up a successful career because you refused to give up your faith, even though many of your friends did. Help us not to give in to the bad example of others.

Chorus 1   Lord, make us instruments of your peace.

Chorus 2   Where there is hatred, let us sow love. Where there is doubt, let us sow faith.

Reader 1   May we always give good example to younger children by choosing to live our faith fully.

Chorus 1   Lord, make us instruments of your peace.

Chorus 2   Where there is hatred, let us sow love. Where there is doubt, let us sow faith.

Prayer Response

Take time now to pray for people the children know who serve in the military, that they may make good and unselfish decisions. The response is: "St. Sebastian, pray for us." Conclude with a few moments of silent prayer.

Action Response

Invite the children to offer one another a sign of peace. Being peacemakers is a great way of giving witness to their faith. Encourage them to be peacemakers particularly at school and at home through their acts of kindness to others.

Before the children leave, give each an index card on which is written: My Personal Prayer to St. Sebastian. They can take the cards home to complete with help from their parents. Encourage them to say the prayer at bedtime.

Optional Activity

Ask the children if they know some of the duties and responsibilities of people in the military. Is it possible for soldiers to follow Christ? In what ways? Then ask them to come up with a list of ways that people who serve in the military can do great things for God and others.

TEN

Agnes the Teenager

FEASTDAY: January 21

Leader   Agnes, an early Roman martyr (died c. 305), was only thirteen years old when she chose to die rather than give up her desire to follow Jesus. She is often pictured with a lamb, a sign of innocence, but also a sign that she believed that Jesus, the lamb of God, was always with her. St. Agnes is the patron saint of children.

Suggested prayer gesture: *All should place their left hand on their heart as the Chorus lines are recited.*

Chorus 1   O good Jesus, hear me. Within your wounds shelter me.

Chorus 2   From the evil one protect me. Let me praise you with all your saints, forever and ever.

Reader 1   St. Agnes, even though you were only a child, you believed that Jesus was with you. Help us to remember that Jesus is always with us, too.

Chorus 1   O good Jesus, hear me. Within your wounds shelter me.

Chorus 2   From the evil one protect me. Let me praise you with all your saints, forever and ever.

Reader 2   St. Agnes, you refused to give up your faith. Help us to be proud of our faith and to proclaim it daily.

Chorus 1   O good Jesus, hear me. Within your wounds shelter me.

Chorus 2   From the evil one protect me. Let me praise you with all your saints, forever and ever.

Reader 1   St. Agnes, you are the patron saint of children. Watch over us and pray for us, today and always.

Chorus 1   O good Jesus, hear me. Within your wounds shelter me.

Chorus 2   From the evil one protect me. Let me praise you with all your saints, forever and ever.

Prayer Response

Take time now to pray for children throughout the world who are affected by war, famine, or illnesses. The response is: "St. Agnes, pray for us." Conclude with a few moments of silent prayer.

Action Response

Give each child a small card that says: "May you live your faith today." Discuss how they might do this and offer them some concrete suggestions. For example: remembering to pray, treating others kindly, helping someone in need, obeying parents and teachers, respecting the rights (and toys, books, games, etc.) of others.

Before the children leave, give each an index card on which is written: My Personal Prayer to St. Agnes. They can take the cards home to complete with help from their parents. Encourage them to say the prayer at bedtime.

Optional Activity

Lead the children in the following guided meditation, pausing briefly after each sentence:

Close your eyes, and breathe deeply five times…. Keep very still and feel your body slowing down, being quiet…. Now think about St. Agnes, a young girl who chose to follow Jesus, even though her life was in danger…. Talk to Jesus now for a few minutes about your own life…. Do you make choices that Jesus would be proud of?… How can he help you to be strong?… What do you need most from him right now?… Talk to him about these things in silence.

(After three minutes or so, have the children open their eyes.)

ELEVEN

Christopher

FEASTDAY: July 25

Leader   Christopher lived in the third century, and his name means "Christ bearer." Legend has it that he was carrying a small child across a river and the child grew heavier and heavier. When he reached the other side, the child revealed that he was Jesus Christ, and he was so heavy because he was carrying the problems of the world.

Suggested prayer gesture: *All should bow deeply before each of the Side 1/Side 2 prayers are prayed.*

Side 1   God, you are the giver of all life.

Side 2   We ask you today to guide us and help us with our problems.

Reader 1   St. Christopher, pray for us that we might always try to love and serve others, especially those who are carrying heavy crosses.

Side 1   God, you are the giver of all life.

Side 2   We ask you today to guide us and help us with our problems.

Reader 2   St. Christopher, help us to remember that when we help those in need, we are helping Jesus, just as you did by carrying him so carefully on your back.

Side 1   God, you are the giver of all life.

Side 2   We ask you today to guide us and help us with our problems.

Reader 3   Pray for us, Christ-Bearer, that God will give us the courage to reach out to others.

Side 1   God, you are the giver of all life.

Side 2   We ask you today to guide us and help us with our problems.

Prayer Response

At this time, the children can pray aloud for those in our world who are overwhelmed by their difficulties, especially children who are sick with serious illnesses. All can respond: "St. Christopher, pray for us all." Invite the children to also pray for personal needs and concerns. Conclude with a moment of silent prayer.

Action Response

Explain to the children that often we feel helpless when people we know are carrying heavy burdens. Discuss ways that they can do small things that really make a difference. Offer practical examples like: smiling at an unpopular child; helping a sibling with homework; calling a lonely neighbor; writing thank-you notes; complimenting others for even the small things they do well.

Before the children leave, give each an index card on which is written: My Personal Prayer to St. Christopher. They can take the cards home to complete with help from their parents. Encourage them to say the prayer at bedtime.

Optional Activity

Explain to the children that some people carry St. Christopher medals or medallions in their cars, hoping for a safe journey. Teach the children this short prayer, one they can say whenever they enter a vehicle (e.g., family car, school bus, train, plane).

> Dear Jesus, be with us as we travel.
> Keep us safe and free from care.
> St. Christopher, give us a safe journey.
> This is our hope and this is our prayer.

TWELVE

Martin of Tours

FEASTDAY: November 11

Leader Martin of Tours (316-397) was a soldier in the Roman army. One cold night a beggar was freezing and Martin gave him half his cloak. Later in a dream he saw Jesus wearing the cloak. He left the army, became a Christian, and was eventually made a bishop.

Suggested prayer gesture: *All should hold hands as Reader parts are prayed.*

All Jesus, our savior and brother, may your peace take root in our hearts and bring forth a harvest of love, holiness, and truth.

Reader 1 St. Martin, you were a good and generous person who shared what you had with the poor. Help us to share as you did.

All Jesus, our savior and brother, may your peace take root in our hearts and bring forth a harvest of love, holiness, and truth.

Reader 2	St. Martin, help us to give up things that are not good for us, so that we might have more money to share with those who are poor and in need.
All	Jesus, our savior and brother, may your peace take root in our hearts and bring forth a harvest of love, holiness, and truth.
Reader 3	St. Martin, help us as a class to do what we can to reach out to those in our parish who are sick or lonely or in need in any way.
All	Jesus, our savior and brother, may your peace take root in our hearts and bring forth a harvest of love, holiness, and truth.

Prayer Response

At this time, invite the children to spend a few minutes in silence thinking about people they know or know about who are in special need of prayer. After two minutes or so, invite them to pray aloud for these people and for their own needs and intentions. All can respond: "St. Martin of Tours, pray for us." Conclude with a moment of silent prayer.

Action Response

If you have time, allow the children to dramatize the story of Martin giving his coat to a beggar and then seeing the coat on Jesus. Encourage creativity. Before they leave, ask the children to go through their closets at home and find at least one (in good condition) toy or piece of clothing that they can share with someone in need.

Before the children leave, give each an index card on which is written: My Personal Prayer to St. Martin of Tours. They can take the cards home to complete with help from their parents. Encourage them to say the prayer at bedtime.

Optional Activity

Share this story with your class.

In a dream, an old woman heard Christ Jesus say that he would visit her on Christmas day. She had no family and thus she was overjoyed that she would have Christ himself for company. She prepared the best meal possible and she cleaned her little house until it shone.

Christmas day came and the woman was up early, waiting. She quickly answered a knock at the door, but it was only a neighbor child begging a bit of milk for his sick mother. Now there would be no milk for Jesus, the old woman thought, but she gave it anyway. At noon, another knock. This time it was an elderly couple whose car had stalled. They were very hungry and so, while they waited for help, the woman gave them part of her well-planned supper. By early evening Christ had still not come.

But then there was a third knock at the door. Excited the woman opened it to a teenage girl who had run from home after a fight with her parents. She was cold and her feet were muddy. Into the clean room she came, tracking mud on the gleaming floor. The old woman sat her by the fire, gave her the remainder of the special meal, and listened to her story. Then she called the parents who came and took their daughter safely home.

That night as she lay in her bed, the old woman prayed, "Why didn't you come to me, Christ Jesus? I waited all day for you." As she drifted off to sleep, she heard a voice say, "Oh, but I came three times, and each time you received me. How blessed are you, my friend. Sleep well."

THIRTEEN

Monica

FEASTDAY: August 27

Leader	Monica (332-387) is best known as the mother of St. Augustine, who had at one time turned his back on God. Monica prayed for many years that he would become a Christian. She never gave up hope and her son was finally baptized. She is the patron saint of mothers.

Suggested prayer gesture: *All should fold their hands as the Reader parts are prayed.*

Chorus 1	Loving God, we believe in you and we trust in you.
Chorus 2	We love you above all things.
Reader 1	St. Monica, we ask you to pray for us, just as you prayed for your son. May we grow in faith and always trust that God is guiding us.
Chorus 1	Loving God, we believe in you and we trust in you.

Chorus 2 We love you above all things.

Reader 2 St. Monica, help us to be true Christians, who reach out to others in Jesus' name.

Chorus 1 Loving God, we believe in you and we trust in you.

Chorus 2 We love you above all things.

Reader 3 St. Monica, just as your son Augustine eventually turned his life over to God, may we too turn to God and grow in faith.

Chorus 1 Loving God, we believe in you and we trust in you.

Chorus 2 We love you above all things.

Prayer Response

At this time, invite the children to pray aloud for all parents that they may be models of faith for their children. All can respond: "St. Monica, pray for parents." Remind the children to include parents who live in very poor nations who are not able to give their children even the basic necessities of life. Conclude with a moment of silent prayer.

Action Response

Are there any symbols of your faith (a crucifix, prayer table, a Bible, etc.) in your teaching space? If not, decide as a class where in the room you will gather for prayer and ask the children to help you decorate it with drawings. Encourage them to take turns bringing items from home for future classes to place on your prayer table.

Before the children leave, give each an index card on which is written: My Prayer to St. Monica. They can take the cards home to complete with help from their parents. Encourage them to say the prayer at bedtime.

Optional Activity

St. Monica is an example of a parent with great faith who believed in the power of prayer. It took many, many years for her prayers to be answered, but she never gave up. Her son not only became a Christian, but was also a famous one. In today's world, children are used to instant gratification, even in their prayer. To help them get a sense of time in God's eyes, try the following activity:

Prepare strips of paper with prayer intentions on them and have each child take one, read it, and then share how long they think it might take to have the prayer answered. Sample prayer intentions can include: help my grandmother to get well; give me a good grade on my math test; let there be peace in our world; help my dad find a job; let Christmas come sooner than usual; help my little sister to stop annoying me. Add others that seem appropriate for your group. Explain that things happen in God's good time and not all prayers are answered immediately or in the way we wish.

FOURTEEN

Genevieve the Brave

FEASTDAY: January 3

Leader	St. Genevieve (420-500) is known for her deep faith and the way she prayed, always believing in God's help. Once when a barbarian tribe was about to attack Paris, Genevieve prayed day and night, and the tribe did not attack. We, too, must have faith in the power of our prayer.

Suggested prayer gesture: *All should hold their right hands upward as the Chorus prayers are recited.*

Chorus 1	Loving God, we cannot exist without you.
Chorus 2	Help us to think and act rightly.
Reader 1	Guide us, St. Genevieve, that we might turn to God in times of trouble as you did. Help us to believe that God will hear our prayers.
Chorus 1	Loving God, we cannot exist without you.

Chorus 2   Help us to think and act rightly.

Reader 2   We ask you, loving God, to remember all our needs. Keep us free from harm and help us to grow in faith.

Chorus 1   Loving God, we cannot exist without you.

Chorus 2   Help us to think and act rightly.

Reader 3   We ask you to remember all those for whom we have promised to pray. May we always think of others and do what we can to help them and may we pray daily for our country and our world.

Chorus 1   Loving God, we cannot exist without you.

Chorus 2   Help us to think and act rightly.

Prayer Response

At this time, the children can pray aloud for war-torn countries and the people who live in them. Encourage them to especially pray for the children in these countries. All can respond: "St. Genevieve, pray for world peace." Also allow time for the children to pray for personal needs and concerns. Conclude with a moment of silent prayer.

Action Response

As a class, choose a particular area of our world that is facing war, famine, or other serious disasters. Make this area the focus of your class prayer for a month or more. Remind the children of the power of prayer and the need to pray not just for themselves, but for all people everywhere.

Before the children leave, give each an index card on which is written: My Personal Prayer to St. Genevieve. They can take the cards home to complete with help from their parents. Encourage them to say the prayer at bedtime.

Optional Activity

Though the children see news reports of wars, famines, floods, and so on, they don't necessarily take time to consider the people going through them, much less pray for them. The following guided meditation is a quick way to put the children in touch with what others are experiencing. After the children are quiet (eyes shut, slow breathing), say:

Your name is María and you live in Central America. There has been a great flood and your house was washed away. Your family is living in a tent now and there is not much food. What do you want to say to God? (Allow time for silent prayer.)

Your name is Fredric and you live in Eastern Europe. There has been fighting for a long time, but the guns are quiet now. Your parents have forbidden you go play in the field though because of the land mines. What do you want to say to God? (Allow time for silent prayer.)

Invite the children to discuss this experience afterward.

FIFTEEN

Brendan the Navigator

FEASTDAY: May 16

Leader   Brendan the Navigator (486-575) spent his childhood in the care of St. Ita, and from her he learned to live a simple life and to be generous with his love for others. He founded many monasteries in Ireland. Because he was a missionary, he was often traveling on the water and thus is called the navigator saint.

Suggested prayer gesture: *All should kneel as the Reader parts are prayed.*

Chorus 1   Sing joyfully to the Lord, all you lands.

Chorus 2   Serve the Lord with gladness.

Chorus 3   Come before God singing with joy.

Reader 1   St. Brendan, you learned to value your faith when you were only a child. Help us to grow in faith and generous love.

Chorus 1	Sing joyfully to the Lord, all you lands.
Chorus 2	Serve the Lord with gladness.
Chorus 3	Come before God singing with joy.
Reader 2	St. Brendan, you valued the teachings of Ita. Help us to learn from and value our parents and teachers.
Chorus 1	Sing joyfully to the Lord, all you lands.
Chorus 2	Serve the Lord with gladness.
Chorus 3	Come before God singing with joy.
Reader 3	St. Brendan, help all parents to teach their children well and to be models of faith for them. Pray for our parents and grandparents, and for all who guide us.
Chorus 1	Sing joyfully to the Lord, all you lands.
Chorus 2	Serve the Lord with gladness.
Chorus 3	Come before God singing with joy.

Prayer Response

Take time now to pray for your class' special needs as students, and remind the children to also pray for their parents and teachers, including religion teachers. The response is: "St. Brendan, pray for us." End with a moment of silent prayer.

Action Response

St. Brendan spent time in a boat and had many adventures on the water. Use water today to remind the children of their call to be Christians. Bless each one with holy water by making a cross on each person's forehead.

Before the children leave, give each an index card on which is written: My Personal Prayer to St. Brendan. They can take the cards home to complete with help from their parents. Encourage them to say the prayer at bedtime.

Optional Activity

St. Brendan was from County Kerry in Ireland and grew up with water all around. If possible, show the children a map of Ireland and point out some of the waterways that Brendan may have traveled. It is said that he once went as far as North America, which he called the Isles of the Blessed.

SIXTEEN

Gregory the Great

FEASTDAY: September 3

Leader   Gregory the Great (540-604) was a very talented spiritual leader and was widely admired for his intelligence and his devotion to the church. He wrote music that is known today as Gregorian chant. He called himself the servant of the servants of God.

Suggested prayer gesture: *All should fold hands (as in praying hands) as Reader parts are prayed.*

Chorus 1   Remember, dear God, all of us gathered here before you.

Chorus 2   You know how firmly we believe in you.

Chorus 3   We dedicate ourselves to you this day and always.

Reader 1   We thank you, loving God, for the gift of our faith and for the gift of the church. Help us to support one another by loving service and prayer.

Chorus 1   Remember, dear God, all of us gathered here before you.

Chorus 2   You know how firmly we believe in you.

Chorus 3   We dedicate ourselves to you this day and always.

Reader 2   Help us to get to know you better this Lent by going to Mass, receiving the sacraments, and reflecting often on Scripture.

Chorus 1   Remember, dear God, all of us gathered here before you.

Chorus 2   You know how firmly we believe in you.

Chorus 3   We dedicate ourselves to you this day and always.

Reader 3   We ask you, St. Gregory the Great, to pray for us that we might be true followers of Jesus Christ.

Chorus 1   Remember, dear God, all of us gathered here before you.

Chorus 2   You know how firmly we believe in you.

Chorus 3   We dedicate ourselves to you this day and always.

Prayer Response

Take time now to pray for all church leaders, your pastor and parish staff, your bishop, and especially the pope. The response is: "St. Gregory the Great, pray for our church leaders." Encourage the children to also pray for their own needs and those of family and friends. End with a moment of silent prayer.

Action Response

Invite the children to come to your next class prepared to share an example of their favorite music and why they like it. They can sing part of this music, record it on a tape, or give a brief description of it and what attracts them to it. If possible, play a Gregorian chant for your class.

Before the children leave, give each an index card on which is written: My Personal Prayer to St. Gregory the Great. They can take the cards home to complete with help from their parents. Encourage them to say the prayer at bedtime.

Optional Activity

Have your class compose a chant of praise to God. Decide as a class how many verses the chant will have and then let small groups work on writing the verses. When all have completed the verses, practice reciting them in plainchant, or ask your parish music director to visit your class and help the children put their verses to song.

SEVENTEEN

Gertrude of Nivelles

FEASTDAY: March 17

Leader   Gertrude of Nivelles (626-659) was born in Belgium and became a nun when she was fourteen years old. Eventually she was appointed Abbess (the religious leader) of the abbey. She was well known for her hospitality to travelers, and she treated strangers as if they were family. Let us imitate her generosity.

Suggested prayer gesture: *All should extend both arms outward and upward as Reader parts are prayed.*

Left Side   Blessed is our God at all times.

Right Side   Generous is our God, now and always, forever and ever.

Reader 1   St. Gertrude, please pray for us that we might be happy to share our lives with all those who visit us or need our care and concern.

Left Side   Blessed is our God at all times.

Right Side   Generous is our God, now and always, forever and ever.

Reader 2   Jesus, you tell us in the gospel that what we do for others, we do for you. Help us to do this willingly and generously.

Left Side   Blessed is our God at all times.

Right Side   Generous is our God, now and always, forever and ever.

Reader 3   St. Gertrude, thank you for your example of welcoming others in Jesus' name. Guide us as we try to do the same.

Left Side   Blessed is our God at all times.

Right Side   Generous is our God, now and always, forever and ever.

Prayer Response

Take time now for spontaneous prayer. If there are special needs the children have, encourage them to pray for these and also to remember those who are suffering throughout the world, especially the homeless. The response is: "St. Gertrude, pray for us." End with a few minutes of silent prayer.

Action Response

Read and discuss Matthew 25:31–46 with your class. Then give each child a slip of paper on which the following is written: Be friendly to everyone you meet today. Be especially pleasant to those who are sad or lonely. Remember Jesus' words: "What you do for others, you do for me."

Before the children leave, give each an index card on which is written: My Personal Prayer to St. Gertrude. They can take the cards home to complete with help from their parents. Encourage them to say the prayer at bedtime.

Optional Activity

If possible, invite a religious sister to speak to your class about the work her community does. Prepare the children beforehand by talking about religious life as a call from God. Explain that religious communities were begun to do certain works in the church: some to teach, or nurse, or work with the poor, etc. Encourage them to ask the visitor who founded her community and for what purpose.

EIGHTEEN

Clare of Assisi

FEASTDAY: August 11

Leader   Clare of Assisi (1194-1253) grew up in a wealthy family, but she chose to live a life of extreme poverty and depended on the gifts of others to survive. If she and her followers received more than they needed, they always gave it to the poor. Clare was a disciple of St. Francis of Assisi.

Suggested prayer gesture: *All should take one step forward as the Side One lines are prayed and one step back as the Side Two lines are recited.*

Side 1   In all our trials, Lord, walk with us; in all our trials walk with us.

Side 2   When our hearts are almost breaking, we want Jesus to walk with us.

Reader 1   St. Clare, you had every chance to live a wealthy and luxurious life, but you chose to live in service to others. Help us to depend more on God than on material things for happiness.

Side 1   In all our trials, Lord, walk with us; in all our trials walk with us.

Side 2   When our hearts are almost breaking, we want Jesus to walk with us.

Reader 2   St. Clare, pray for us that we might share our money and our belongings with those in need.

Side 1   In all our trials, Lord, walk with us; in all our trials walk with us.

Side 2   When our hearts are almost breaking, we want Jesus to walk with us.

Reader 3   St. Clare, help us today and always to pray often and to share generously.

Side 1   In all our trials, Lord, walk with us; in all our trials walk with us.

Side 2   When our hearts are almost breaking, we want Jesus to walk with us.

Prayer Response

Take time now to pray for your class' special needs, and remember to pray for people living in poverty throughout our world. The response is: "St. Clare, pray for us." End with a moment of silent prayer.

Action Response

Invite each child to contribute money of his or her own in your next class to help feed a child who comes to your local soup kitchen. If the children have no money, ask them to pray for children who are in need. During your prayer time, for example, lead a litany of petition for children throughout the world who are suffering in any way.

Before the children leave, give each an index card on which is written: My Personal Prayer to St. Clare. They can take the cards home to complete with help from their parents. Encourage them to say the prayer at bedtime.

Optional Activity

Explain to the children that St. Clare was a close associate of Francis of Assisi. Clare had once been a wealthy young woman, but she gave up her luxurious way of life to devote herself to Christ and the poor. The religious community she founded was known as the Poor Clares. Invite the children to take home the following three questions to be answered with help from their parents.

1) Why would anyone give up comfortable living and make the choice to live in poverty?

2) Are there any people alive today who make this kind of choice? Who are they?

3) Can you imagine ever making such a choice? What or who would make you want to do it?

NINETEEN

Albert the Great

FEASTDAY: November 15

Leader Albert the Great (1206-1280) was a dedicated scholar who had an interest in many different subjects. He reminds us that we are all learners (even teachers), and he reminds children that being a student is their particular call from God.

Suggested prayer gesture: *All should bow their heads slightly as the Chorus parts are prayed.*

Chorus 1 Lord Jesus Christ, keep us faithful to your teaching.

Chorus 2 Never let us be parted from you.

Reader 1 St. Albert the Great, help us as a class to continue to open our minds and hearts to God's Word that we may learn more and more about following Jesus.

Chorus 1 Lord Jesus Christ, keep us faithful to your teaching.

Chorus 2   Never let us be parted from you.

Reader 2   St. Albert the Great, please pray that we will be the best students we can be and thus work hard at school and in religion class to learn as much as possible.

Chorus 1   Lord Jesus Christ, keep us faithful to your teaching.

Chorus 2   Never let us be parted from you.

All   May we be good students
as God wants us to be.
Pray for us, St. Albert,
that God's will we might see.

Prayer Response

Take time now to pray for special needs your parish has, and ask the children to pray for students all over the world. Ask them, too, to pray for children who are not able to go school for whatever reasons. The response is: "St. Albert the Great, pray for us." Conclude with a few moments of silence.

Action Response

Remind the children that their vocation is to be students, the best students they can be. Discuss the fact that God calls all of us to a vocation, and for children a large part of their vocation is to study. Bless each child as they leave class by making the sign of the cross on their foreheads while saying: "May God help you with your studies."

Before the children leave, give each an index card on which is written: My Personal Prayer to St. Albert. They can take the cards home to complete with help from their parents. Encourage them to say the prayer at bedtime.

Optional Activity

Play this vocation game with your class. Make a list of all the occupations you can think of, for example: scholars and researchers (like St. Albert), mechanics, farmers, nurses, teachers, religious sisters and brothers, politicians, lawyers, parents, doctors, priests, stockbrokers, race car drivers, electricians, students, singers, and so on. Write these occupations/vocations on separate slips of paper.

Divide the class into two teams. Team one takes a slip and reads what it says to team two. Team two has ten seconds to come up with one concrete way a person in that occupation can be holy (through the work they do). Each team gets a point for answering on time. The team with the most points wins. After this game, talk about how all of us are called to excel at what we do. Holiness comes with doing our best and looking out for others.

TWENTY

Elizabeth of Portugal

FEASTDAY: July 4

Leader   Elizabeth of Portugal (1271-1336) was the daughter of a king and was forced to marry a neighboring king when she was only twelve years old. She had two children, but her husband was unfaithful. Elizabeth did not yield to self-pity, but rather spent her time caring for the poor and the sick as well as for her two children.

Suggested prayer gesture: *Everyone should bow their heads as the All parts are prayed.*

All   Loving God, we cannot exist without you.

Side 1   Help us to think and act rightly,

Side 2   And may we always live as you want us to live.

Reader 1   Help us, God our Father, to make sacrifices for one another and to help one another in every way possible.

All   Loving God, we cannot exist without you.

Side 1   Help us to think and act rightly,

Side 2   And may we always live as you want us to live.

Reader 2   When we have problems in our class, be with us, Jesus, our savior, and help us to find peaceful solutions.

All   Loving God, we cannot exist without you.

Side 1   Help us to think and act rightly,

Side 2   And may we always live as you want us to live.

Reader 3   When there is sickness or injury in our lives, Holy Spirit, help us to offer one another love and joy. Help us to always offer one another forgiveness.

All   Loving God, we cannot exist without you.

Side 1   Help us to think and act rightly,

Side 2   And may we always live as you want us to live.

Prayer Response

Take time now to pray for your special needs, and remember to pray for families throughout the world. The response is: "St. Elizabeth, pray for us." End with a few moments of silent prayer.

Action Response

Remembering that all of us sometimes hurt one another, encourage the children to offer one another forgiveness today by sharing a Sign of Peace at the end of class.

Before the children leave, give each an index card on which is written: My Personal Prayer to St. Elizabeth. They can take the cards home to complete with help from their parents. Encourage them to say the prayer at bedtime.

Optional Activity

Children today are heavily influenced by the cultural practices advanced by the media. It is commonplace for them to see sexual relationships among the unmarried and infidelity in marriages. It is also commonplace that divorce is clearly an option. Take this opportunity to talk about marriage today and ways that people might work through some of their problems instead of resorting to divorce. If possible, invite a member of your parish staff or a marriage counselor to visit your class to talk about the sacred bond of marriage.

TWENTY-ONE

Catherine of Siena

FEASTDAY: April 29

Leader   Catherine of Siena (1347-1380) was an attractive and lively girl, but at an early age she decided to devote herself to prayer and penance. She had a strong personality and often converted known sinners. Once she even scolded the pope for moving from Rome to France to get away from the troubles there. The pope listened to Catherine and returned to Rome.

Suggested prayer gesture: *All should kneel as the Reader parts are prayed.*

Reader 1   Stay with us, Lord Jesus, for the evening draws near, and be our companion along the way.

Reader 2   Set our hearts on fire with your holy word.

Leader   Jesus, help us to dedicate ourselves to you. Help us to love and serve others in your name as St.

Catherine of Siena did.

Reader 1   Stay with us, Lord Jesus, for the evening draws near, and be our companion along the way.

Reader 2   Set our hearts on fire with your holy word.

Leader   Jesus, help us to be strong in our faith and to believe that you are always with us, in all our joys and sorrows.

Reader 1   Stay with us, Lord Jesus, for the evening draws near, and be our companion along the way.

Reader 2   Set our hearts on fire with your holy word.

Leader   Catherine of Siena, pray for us today and always, that we might work together to follow Jesus.

Reader 1   Stay with us, Lord Jesus, for the evening draws near, and be our companion along the way.

Reader 2   Set our hearts on fire with your holy word.

Prayer Response

Take time now to pray for religious people all over the world, and also invite the children to pray for their own special needs. The response is: "St. Catherine of Siena, pray for us." End with a few moments of silent prayer.

Action Response

Fasting is a traditional practice in the church, one that was practiced by Catherine of Siena. Encourage the children to "fast" today from criticizing others, name calling, fighting, and any other behavior that might harm another. Encourage them to offer kind words to others rather than critical or harsh ones.

Before the children leave, give each an index card on which is written: My Personal Prayer to St. Catherine of Siena. They can take the cards home to complete with help from their parents. Encourage them to say the prayer at bedtime.

Optional Activity

Remind the children that Catherine had very strong convictions and was a person of deep prayer. She relied on the guidance of the Holy Spirit, so much so that she was able to call the pope to task for not relying on God's help. Invite the children to talk about the pope we have today. What might Catherine say to him? Invite the children to write to the pope to share with him how they feel about being Catholic and what their hopes are for the church.

TWENTY-TWO

Frances of Rome

FEASTDAY: March 9

Leader   Frances of Rome (1384-1440) wife and mother, was married for forty years. During all that time, besides attending to her household duties and caring for her children, she cared for the poor and visited the sick. Many women joined her in this work, which continues today.

Suggested prayer gesture: *Everyone should bow heads as the All prayers are prayed.*

Right Side   Jesus, redeemer of the world, we are yours and yours we wish always to be.

Left Side   Praise to you, our savior and our king.

Reader 1   St. Frances, bless us and pray for us that we might reach out to the poor and the sick.

All   Show us how to follow Jesus day by day, in every way.

Right Side   Jesus, redeemer of the world, we are yours and yours we wish always to be.

Left Side   Praise to you, our savior and our king.

Reader 2   St. Frances, help us to love and serve one another, through listening to one another and helping one another to grow in faith.

All   Show us how to follow Jesus day by day, in every way.

Right Side   Jesus, redeemer of the world, we are yours and yours we wish always to be.

Left Side   Praise to you, our savior and our king.

Reader 3   Bless our parents, St. Frances, that they might be good guides. Bless us that we might love and respect our parents, teachers, and other leaders who guide us in any way.

All   Show us how to follow Jesus day by day, in every way.

Prayer Response

At this time, the children can pray aloud for all those who are sick, people they know and people they don't know throughout the world. Also encourage them to pray for doctors and nurses and all hospital personnel. All can respond: "St. Frances of Rome, cure our ills." Conclude with a moment of silent prayer.

Action Response

As a class, send a get-well card to someone in the parish who is sick. If you don't know anyone personally, check your parish bulletin for names of sick parishioners. Have each child sign the card, and remind the children to pray for this person in their bedtime prayers at home.

Before the children leave, give each an index card on which is written: My Personal Prayer to St. Frances. They can take the cards home to complete with help from their parents. Encourage them to say the prayer at bedtime.

Optional Activity

If possible arrange for your class to visit a local nursing home to bring drawings to the residents. Prepare the children beforehand by talking about some of the illnesses the people may have. Explain that sick people, as well as all others, are children of God who deserve our care and respect.

TWENTY-THREE

Martin de Porres

FEASTDAY: November 3

Leader   Martin de Porres (1579-1639) was a simple and holy man. He was born in Peru of a Spanish father and an African mother, and he experienced prejudice because of his dark skin. He did all he could to ease the suffering of the slaves who were shipped to Peru from Africa. He was so kind that he was called "father of charity."

Suggested prayer gesture: *All should place a hand over their hearts as the All prayers are said.*

All   Jesus, gentle and humble of heart, touch our hearts and make them like your own.

Reader 1   Martin de Porres, you imitated Jesus in so many ways, especially by your love and concern for others. Pray for us, that we might imitate Jesus too.

All   Jesus, gentle and humble of heart, touch our hearts and make them like your own.

Reader 2   St. Martin, you helped victims of injustice, especially the slaves. Pray for us that we too might reach out to those who suffer.

All   Jesus, gentle and humble of heart, touch our hearts and make them like your own.

Reader 1   Jesus, forgive us for the times we have looked down on others, and teach us to love and respect people of all races, ages, genders, and creeds.

All   Jesus, gentle and humble of heart, touch our hearts and make them like your own.

Prayer Response

At this time, the children can pray aloud for all those in our world who are victims of injustice and prejudice. All can respond: "St. Martin de Porres, change our hearts." Also give the children time to pray for their own particular needs and concerns. Conclude with a moment of silent prayer.

Action Response

Before class, prepare strips of paper with the following words on them: Asian, Jewish, fat, skinny, black, white, tall, old, sick, handicapped, and any other words that your group might associate with prejudice. Spend a few minutes in class talking about prejudice and the harm it can do. Have each child choose one of the slips (from a basket or bowl), and then ask the children to silently consider what they feel when they read the word. End this activity by again praying: "St. Martin de Porres, change our hearts."

Before the children leave, give each an index card on which is written: My Personal Prayer to St. Martin de Porres. They can take the cards home to complete with help from their parents. Encourage them to say the prayer at bedtime.

Optional Activity

If your particular group shows signs of prejudice, try the following activity. Using the same strips as above, have the children take turns drawing one from the basket or bowl. Each child should pretend to be the person on the card and give a brief presentation to the rest of the class, explaining why others should accept him or her as a child of God. A "handicapped" person, for example, might want to tell the group how he or she feels when others ignore him or her, and that having a handicap doesn't mean you are stupid or unfeeling. When all have had a turn, invite the children to discuss how they felt during these presentations.

TWENTY-FOUR

Peter Claver

FEASTDAY: September 9

Leader   Peter Claver (1580-1654) was born in Spain, but he spent much of his life as a missionary in South America, where he helped care for more than 300,000 slaves. He gave them medicine, food, and drink, and he treated them as friends.

Suggested prayer gesture: *Everyone should kneel when the All parts are recited.*

All   Help us, loving God, to give our love and care to others, especially those in need.

Reader 1   St. Peter Claver, you were from a rich family, but you gave up your wealth to serve the poorest of the poor. Teach us to care for the poor and the hungry.

All   Help us, loving God, to give our love and care to others, especially those in need.

Reader 2   St. Peter Claver, you gave up your homeland to work with people who were strangers. Help us to offer kindness to every one we meet today.

All   Help us, loving God, to give our love and care to others, especially those in need.

Reader 1   Jesus, we ask you, please, to help us to be as generous as Peter Claver was. May we see you today in every person we meet, and especially in those who are sad or lonely.

All   Help us, loving God, to give our love and care to others, especially those in need.

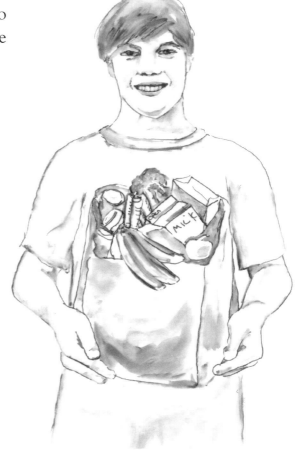

Prayer Response

Take time now for spontaneous prayer. Ask the children to remember those suffering throughout the world, especially those who do not have the gift of freedom. If there are special needs the children have, pray for them at this time as well. The response is: "St. Peter Claver, pray for us." End with a few minutes of silent prayer.

Action Response

Today in many parts of the world, people are refugees because of war, ethnic disputes, and famine. As a class, pray for all the dedicated people who help refugees: doctors, nurses, missionaries, and the like. Also pray for the refugees themselves. If your parish or diocese supports missionaries, have the children write a note of thanks to one of them, asking for information about their ministry.

Before the children leave, give each an index card on which is written: My Personal Prayer to St. Peter Claver. They can take the cards home to complete with help from their parents. Encourage them to say the prayer at bedtime.

Optional Activity

Explain to the children that still in our day there are people who do extraordinary ministries. Talk about Mother Teresa and her community, for example. Or share with them information about Dorothy Day, Bishop Oscar Romero, Thomas Merton, or the spiritual writer Henri Nouwen. If there are people in your parish or diocese who are involved in special outreach ministries, share this information with your class as well.

TWENTY-FIVE

Vincent de Paul

FEASTDAY: September 27

Leader   Vincent de Paul (1581-1660) was known for his charitable work for the poor, the imprisoned, and soldiers wounded in war. Today his followers continue this work. Many parishes have a Vincent de Paul Society, an organization that helps the poor. They collect food and clothing and provide meals for people in need.

Suggested prayer gesture: *All should raise their left hands as the Chorus parts are prayed.*

Chorus 1   Eternal God, may we your people enjoy health in mind and body, and may our faith in you keep growing.

Chorus 2   May we share our daily bread so that others may eat.

Reader 1   St. Vincent de Paul, you always shared what you had with the needy. Help us to do the same so the suffering of others may cease.

Chorus 1   Eternal God, may we your people enjoy health in mind and body, and may our faith in you keep growing.

Chorus 2   May we share our daily bread so that others may eat.

Reader 2   Help us, St. Vincent, to also share our time with one another, with our friends and neighbors, and with those who are in need.

Chorus 1   Eternal God, may we your people enjoy health in mind and body, and may our faith in you keep growing.

Chorus 2   May we share our daily bread so that others may eat.

Reader 3   Show us, St. Vincent, how to use our talents, our special gifts, and our abilities, to give joy to those around us.

Chorus 1   Eternal God, may we your people enjoy health in mind and body, and may our faith in you keep growing.

Chorus 2   May we share our daily bread so that others may eat.

Prayer Response

At this time, the children can pray aloud for the poor in various parts of the world, especially for children who are without the basic necessities of life. All can respond: "St. Vincent de Paul, pray for us and for all God's children." Pray too for personal needs and then conclude with a moment of silent prayer.

Action Response

Decide as a class one way that you can give joy to someone sad or lonely today and throughout this month. Possibilities include: phone calls, letters, visits, and helping with shopping or chores. Encourage the children to actually carry out what they have resolved to do.

Before the children leave, give each an index card on which is written: My Personal Prayer to St. Vincent de Paul. They can take the cards home to complete with help from their parents. Encourage them to say the prayer at bedtime.

Optional Activity

Contact the person in your parish who is head of the Vincent de Paul Society and ask this person to come and talk to the children in your class. If there is no such group in your parish, contact your diocesan director of social services to see how the needs of the poor are met. The point here is to demonstrate to the children that the work of St. Vincent de Paul still goes on, and they can take part in it.

TWENTY-SIX

Joseph of Cupertino

FEASTDAY: September 18

Leader The family of Joseph of Cupertino (1602-1663) was so poor that Joseph was born in a garden shed. He was not very bright as a child and when he wanted to become a monk, he was turned down. He did not give up, however, and eventually he became a Franciscan. It is said that he was sometimes so deeply into prayer that his body lifted from the ground toward God.

Suggested prayer gesture: *Everyone should bow as the All prayers are recited.*

All Jesus, meek and humble of heart, make our hearts like yours.

Reader 1 Jesus, your follower Joseph of Cupertino was a poor and simple man. He used the gifts he had to lead others to you, and he did the best he could.

All Jesus, meek and humble of heart, make our hearts like yours.

Reader 2   Help us, Jesus, to use the gifts and talents you have given us and to do our best at home and at school.

All   Jesus, meek and humble of heart, make our hearts like yours.

Reader 1   Jesus, teach us to always rely on you and to trust that you will be with us in all our daily chores and in all our joys and sorrows.

All   Jesus, meek and humble of heart, make our hearts like yours.

Reader 2   Make us strong, Jesus, that we might never make fun of those who find their studies hard, but rather give them a helping hand.

All   Jesus, meek and humble of heart, make our hearts like yours.

Prayer Response

Take time now to pray for children who have learning disabilities or handicaps that prevent them from learning. Also pray for the special needs your class might have. The response is: "St. Joseph of Cupertino, pray for us." Conclude with a few moments of silent prayer.

Action Response

If there is someone in your program or school who is handicapped or disabled, discuss with the children ways that they can show extra patience and kindness to this person. Divide the children into pairs. Have each pair come up with a situation in which someone is learning disabled, and someone else offers them patience and kindness. If you have time, allow the children to act out these scenarios.

Before the children leave, give each an index card on which is written: My Personal Prayer to St. Joseph of Cupertino. They can take the cards home to complete with help from their parents. Encourage them to say the prayer at bedtime.

Optional Activity

To give the children an experience of how it feels to be handicapped even in a small way, ask volunteers to allow you to tape three of their fingers together with masking tape and then try to write the same assignment as everyone else. Have them describe how it feels to be asked to do as well as everyone else when they obviously cannot. Help the children to reflect together on their need to be understanding and helpful to those who have difficulties.

TWENTY-SEVEN

Vincent Pallotti

FEASTDAY: January 23

Leader   Vincent Pallotti (1795-1850) was a man of great faith. He worked hard to help the poor and suffering. He had many followers: laypeople, priests, and religious. He believed that everyone is called to live the gospel message. Even today, his followers continue the work of the gospel throughout the world.

Suggested prayer gesture: *All should kneel as the Chorus parts are prayed.*

Chorus 1   Lord Jesus, you are the water for which we thirst…

Chorus 2   You are the companion whom we seek.

Reader 1   St. Vincent Pallotti, pray for us that we might be faithful followers of Jesus. Teach us to thirst for the living water that Jesus is always ready to give.

Chorus 1   Lord Jesus, you are the water for which we thirst…

Chorus 2   You are the companion whom we seek.

Reader 2   St. Vincent, help us to accept our call to live the gospel today and always, and to accept Jesus as our personal guide.

Chorus 1   Lord Jesus, you are the water for which we thirst...

Chorus 2   You are the companion whom we seek.

Reader 3   St. Vincent, strengthen us to reach out to those in need and to share our belongings freely and joyfully as you did.

Chorus 1   Lord Jesus, you are the water for which we thirst...

Chorus 2   You are the companion whom we seek.

Prayer Response

At this time, invite the children to pray aloud for personal as well as worldwide needs and concerns. Encourage them to especially remember priests and religious sisters and brothers. All can respond: "St. Vincent Pallotti, pray that we may love God and others." Conclude with a moment of silent prayer.

Action Response

St. Vincent Pallotti made every effort not to waste anything because he felt that everything could be used to help someone else. He wouldn't even waste a piece of paper! Encourage the children to make every effort this week not to waste food, time, attention, paper, books, pencils, and the like.

Before the children leave, give each an index card on which is written: My Personal Prayer to St. Vincent Pallotti. They can take the cards home to complete with help from their parents. Encourage them to say the prayer at bedtime.

Optional Activity

When his followers asked Vincent Pallotti to write some rules for them, he would not do it because he believed that the gospels were sufficient as a rule of life. Invite your class to go through one of the four gospels and see if they can identify rules that will help them to live as followers of Christ. If your group is large, divide the children into four groups and have each group go through one of the gospels.

TWENTY-EIGHT

John Bosco

FEASTDAY: January 31

Leader　　John Bosco (1815–1888) lived in extreme poverty as a child. When he went off to the seminary, he had to borrow the clothes to wear. His dream was to educate poor children, and he eventually was able to do this. His followers continue his work to this day.

Suggested prayer gesture: *All should kneel each time the Chorus lines are prayed.*

Chorus 1　　Lord Jesus, by your saving death and resurrection, free us from our sins.

Chorus 2　　May your peace take root in our hearts and bring forth a rich harvest of love and truth.

Reader 1　　St. John Bosco, you believed that Jesus would guide you in your life's work of teaching and working with youth. Help us to believe that Jesus is guiding us today.

Chorus 1   Lord Jesus, by your saving death and resurrection, free us from our sins.

Chorus 2   May your peace take root in our hearts and bring forth a rich harvest of love and truth.

Reader 2   St. John, you were very poor and you were very grateful for everything you had. Help us to be grateful for all our gifts, especially for our family and friends.

Chorus 1   Lord Jesus, by your saving death and resurrection, free us from our sins.

Chorus 2   May your peace take root in our hearts and bring forth a rich harvest of love and truth.

Reader 3   St. John, help us to value our education and to use our opportunities to learn and grow with faith and gratitude.

Chorus 1   Lord Jesus, by your saving death and resurrection, free us from our sins.

Chorus 2   May your peace take root in our hearts and bring forth a rich harvest of love and truth.

Prayer Response

Take time now to pray for any special needs your class may have, and encourage the children to pray for students and children living in poverty. The response is: "St. John Bosco, pray for us." End with silent prayer.

Action Response

Give each child in your class a slip of paper and have them write on it the names of any teachers they have or have had that made a special impression on them. Invite them to carry this paper throughout the coming week, and remember to say a prayer for these teachers every day. If they still have one of the teachers, suggest that they thank this teacher for helping them learn.

Before the children leave, give each an index card on which is written: My Personal Prayer to St. John Bosco. They can take the cards home to complete with help from their parents. Encourage them to say the prayer at bedtime.

Optional Activity

Ask one of your parish leaders or a member of your parish social outreach committee to talk to your class about what the parish does to assist the poor, especially poor children. Can he or she suggest at least one realistic way that your class can get involved?

TWENTY-NINE

Thérèse of Lisieux

FEASTDAY October 2

Leader   Thérèse of Lisieux (1873-1897) became a Carmelite nun when she was only fifteen years old. She is called the "Little Flower of Jesus" because she believed that even the smallest act of love is large in the eyes of Jesus. She died of tuberculosis at the age of twenty-four.

Suggested prayer gesture: *Everyone should look skyward as the Left Side prayers are prayed.*

Right Side   Dear Jesus, shine through us and be in us, so that everyone we meet may feel your presence.

Left Side   Let them look up and see no longer us but you.

Reader 1   Jesus, help us to love you as much as Thérèse, your Little Flower, did. Help us to remember that even the smallest acts of love and kindness are important in your eyes.

Right Side   Dear Jesus, shine through us and be in us, so that everyone we meet may feel your presence.

Left Side   Let them look up and see no longer us but you.

Reader 2   Jesus, help us to remember those in need this day and to share with them whatever we can, no matter how small the gift.

Right Side   Dear Jesus, shine through us and be in us, so that everyone we meet may feel your presence.

Left Side   Let them look up and see no longer us but you.

Reader 3   Jesus, help us as a class to offer one another many small acts of kindness and courtesy.

Right Side   Dear Jesus, shine through us and be in us, so that everyone we meet may feel your presence.

Left Side   Let them look up and see no longer us but you.

Prayer Response

Take time now to pray for your class' special needs. Invite the children to also pray for priests and nuns who live in convents and monasteries (as Thérèse did). The response is: "St. Thérèse, pray for us." Conclude with two minutes of silent prayer.

Action Response

As a class, do some small act of kindness for a sick or elderly parishioner today. Have the children write a note or draw a picture for this person. Remind the children that even the smallest acts of love are large in God's eyes.

Before the children leave, give each an index card on which is written: My Personal Prayer to St. Thérèse. They can take the cards home to complete with help from their parents. Encourage them to say the prayer at bedtime.

Optional Activity

Prepare small slips of paper on which are written daily tasks that most children have to perform (one for each child in your group). Have the children draw one out and suggest that they ask God to bless them when they do the task. Possible tasks include: getting up, making the bed, brushing teeth, combing hair, waiting for the school bus, greeting teachers and classmates, listening attentively, and so on.

Maria Goretti

FEASTDAY: July 6

Leader Maria Goretti (1890–1902) was only twelve years old when she was attacked by a neighbor and stabbed to death. She was a happy and cheerful child who was known for her unselfishness and her deep devotion to her faith. Her attacker later was very sorry for what he had done.

Suggested prayer gesture: *All should place their hand near their ear in a listening gesture as the Side One prayers are recited.*

Side 1 Lord Jesus, listen to our prayer and forgive all our sins.

Side 2 Renew your love in our hearts, and help us to be holy children.

Reader 1 St. Maria Goretti, pray for us that we might always choose what is right, no matter how tempted we are to choose sin and selfishness.

Side 1   Lord Jesus, listen to our prayer and forgive all our sins.

Side 2   Renew your love in our hearts, and help us to be holy children.

Reader 2   St. Maria Goretti, pray for our parents and teachers that they might always give good example and show us by their actions that they value their faith.

Side 1   Lord Jesus, listen to our prayer and forgive all our sins.

Side 2   Renew your love in our hearts, and help us to be holy children.

Reader 3   St. Maria Goretti, help us to try to be unselfish and forgiving with one another. Help us to be grateful for the gift of our friends and classmates.

Side 1   Lord Jesus, listen to our prayer and forgive all our sins.

Side 2   Renew your love in our hearts, and help us to be holy children.

Prayer Response

Take time now to pray for teenagers all over the world who are facing temptations. The response is: "St. Maria Goretti, pray for us." Conclude with a moment of silence.

Action Response

Talk to the children about temptation. Explain that all of us are tempted to make selfish choices, but we should try hard to choose what is right. Also explain that we have certain guidelines from the Bible and from the church that help us to make good decisions. (If you have time, make a list of some of these and hand them out: for example, the ten commandments, the beatitudes, sayings of Jesus in the gospels, church laws, and the spiritual and corporal works of mercy.)

Before the children leave, give each an index card on which is written: My Personal Prayer to St. Maria Goretti. They can take the cards home to complete with help from their parents. Encourage them to say the prayer at bedtime.

Optional Activity

Make copies of the following prayer for each child in your class and encourage the children to say this prayer daily:

Thank you, Jesus, for walking with me. I want to be as good as you want me to be. Help me to say "no" to all that is wrong. Give me your blessing that I may be strong. St. Maria Goretti, pray to Jesus for me. Amen.

Suggested Resources

Bunson, Margaret, Matthew, and Stephen; illustrations by Margaret Bunson. *Encyclopedia of Saints.* Our Sunday Visitor Publishing Division, 200 Noll Plaza, Huntington, IN 46750.

Fortosis, Stephen. *Great Men and Women of the Bible.* Paulist Press, 997 Macarthur Boulevard, Mahwah, NJ 07430

Gabriele, Edward F. *Prayer with Searchers and Saints.* St. Mary's Press, 702 Terrace Heights West, Winona, MN 55987.

Glavich, Kathleen. *Saints for All Seasons,* an eight-part video series featuring Francis of Assisi, Martin de Porres, Lucy, Elizabeth Ann Seton, Peter, Joseph, Catherine of Siena, and Isidore. Twenty-Third Publications, P.O. Box 180, Mystic, CT 06355.

Glavich, Kathleen. *Saints for Children: Stories, Activities, Prayer Services.* Twenty-Third Publications, P.O. Box 180, Mystic, CT 06355.

Heffernan, Eileen; illustrated by Jerry Rizzo. *Fifty-seven Saints.* Pauline Books and Media, 50 St. Paul's Ave., Boston, MA 02130.

Neuberger, Anne E. *Mystics & Martyrs, Healers & Hermits, Soldiers & Seekers: Stories of Saints through the Centuries.* Twenty-Third Publications, P.O. Box 180, Mystic, CT 06355.

Schreiber, Gayle. *Saints Alive: Stories and Activities for Young Children.* Twenty-Third Publications, P.O. Box 180, Mystic, CT 06355.

Wallace, Susan Helen; illustrated by Jamie H. Aven. *Saints for Young Readers for Every Day, Volumes 1 and 2.* Pauline Books and Media, 50 St. Paul's Ave., Boston, MA 02130.

Wismar, Gregory J. *Saints and Angels All Around.* Concordia Publishing House, 3558 South Jefferson Ave., St. Louis, MO 63118.

Index of Saints by Month

Of Related Interest...

Saints for Children
Stories, Activities, Prayer Services
Mary Kathleen Glavich, SND

Features 12 popular saints and emphasizes virtues and how middle graders can practice them in their lives. For each saint there is a lively account of his or her life and good works, a prayer service, discussion questions, a craft, activities, and a puzzle or game.

80 pp, $9.95 (order B-40)

Mystics & Martyrs, Healers & Hermits, Soldiers & Seekers...
Stories of Saints through the Centuries
Anne Neuberger

Share with your students (grades 3 to 6) the fascinating story of saints who lived during the 20 centuries of Christianity, with its lights and shadows, its varied situations, problems, and personalities. Included are historical and cultural background information and activities that help children connect the saints' examples to their own lives.

120 pp, $12.95 (order J-31)

Saints for Our Time
Ed Ransom

Presents each saint as a real person, with the same problems, hopes, fears, and dreams as the reader. There are saints for every person and personality, each with a different set of qualities, talents, weaknesses, and attributes. Written in response to the needs of catechumens and RCIA candidates, this volume is recommended reading for every catechist, teacher, student.

304 pp, $14.95 (order B-38)

Book of Saints
Michael Walsh

Here is a saint for each week of the year, some well-known, and some who deserve to be so. Each saint's biography opens with an illuminated capital that depicts a scene or notable quality identified with that saint. These saints can serve to renew our own commitment to faith, prayer, and loving service.

160 pp, $9.95 (order M-20)

Saints Alive
Stories and Activities for Young Children
Gayle Schreiber

Here is a delightful book of short stories illustrating the lives of 30 saints for children in grades pre-K through two. Each story focuses on a positive aspect of the saint's life, offers a prayer to that saint, and includes an activity page.

72 pp, $9.95 (order M-68)

Available at religious bookstores or from:

TWENTY-THIRD PUBLICATIONS

P.O. BOX 180 • 185 WILLOW ST. • MYSTIC, CT 06355 • 1-860-536-2611 • 1-800-321-0411 • FAX 1-800-572-0788

Call for a free catalog